Table of Contents

Introduction..1
Chapter 1: Introduction to Personal Training.....6
Chapter 2: Assessing Your Skills and
Qualifications.. 10
Chapter 3: Understanding Your Target Market.15
Chapter 6: Setting Up Your Business
Operations... 30
Chapter 7: Building Your Brand and Online
Presence.. 36
Chapter 8: Acquiring Clients and Networking. 41
Chapter 9: Providing Exceptional Service........47
Chapter 10: Growing Your Personal Training
Business.. 52

Introduction

Welcome to "The Ultimate Guide on How To Start a Personal Training Business"! This guide is your comprehensive roadmap, designed to help aspiring entrepreneurs like you navigate the journey of starting a successful personal training business. Whether you're passionate about fitness or seeking a rewarding career in the health and wellness industry, this guide will equip you with the knowledge and tools to turn your passion into a thriving business.

Starting a personal training business is both exciting and challenging. It requires a unique mix of fitness expertise, business savvy, and the ability to build strong relationships with clients. With the right strategy, determination, and dedication, you can establish yourself as a trusted fitness professional and build a loyal client base. But before diving into the details of starting your business, let's first explore what personal training is all about and why it's a booming industry.

Chapter 1: Introduction to Personal Training

In Chapter 1, we'll delve into the fascinating world of personal training and its importance in today's health and fitness landscape. We'll discuss the role of a personal trainer, the benefits of personal training, and the various types of clients you might encounter. This chapter will provide you with a solid foundation, helping you understand how personal training can positively impact lives and why it's a lucrative business opportunity.

Chapter 2: Assessing Your Skills and Qualifications

Chapter 2 is all about evaluating your skills and qualifications. Running a successful personal training business requires more than just a passion for fitness; you need the necessary knowledge, expertise, and certifications to provide effective training and guidance. This chapter will guide you through the process of assessing your skills, identifying any gaps, and pursuing the appropriate certifications and training programs to enhance your credibility as a personal trainer.

Chapter 3: Understanding Your Target Market

In Chapter 3, we'll focus on understanding your target market. To build a thriving personal training business, it's crucial to identify and connect with your ideal clients. This chapter will guide you through conducting market research, defining your target audience, and understanding their needs and preferences. By gaining a deep understanding of your target market, you can tailor your services and marketing strategies to attract and retain clients effectively.

Chapter 4: Developing Your Business Plan

Chapter 4 will cover the process of developing a comprehensive business plan for your personal training venture. A well-crafted business plan is essential for setting goals, outlining strategies, and securing financing if needed. This chapter will guide you through the essential components of a business plan, including market analysis, competitive analysis, financial projections, and marketing strategies. Creating a solid business plan will provide you with a roadmap to follow as you launch and grow your personal training business.

Chapter 5: Legal and Regulatory Considerations

Chapter 5 focuses on the critical legal and regulatory considerations when starting a personal training business. From choosing the right legal structure to understanding liability insurance and employment laws, this chapter will ensure that you comply with all necessary legal requirements. Addressing these considerations from the beginning will help protect yourself, your business, and your clients.

Chapter 6: Setting Up Your Business Operations

Chapter 6 will guide you through setting up your business operations. From finding a suitable location to setting up the necessary equipment and software systems, this chapter provides practical insights and tips for creating an efficient and client-friendly environment. Additionally, we'll discuss the importance of securing the right equipment and incorporating technology to streamline your operations.

Chapter 7: Building Your Brand and Online Presence

In Chapter 7, we'll explore the significance of building your brand and establishing a strong online presence. An effective personal training business relies on building trust and credibility with potential clients. This chapter will guide you through defining your brand identity, creating a compelling brand message, and utilizing various online platforms to reach and engage your target audience. By establishing a strong brand and online presence, you can differentiate yourself from the competition and attract more clients.

Chapter 8: Acquiring Clients and Networking

Chapter 8 is dedicated to strategies for acquiring clients and networking. As a personal trainer, acquiring clients is crucial for your business's success. In this chapter, you'll learn effective marketing and promotional strategies to attract and retain clients. We'll discuss the power of referrals, building professional networks, and leveraging social media to expand your client base. Implementing these strategies will help maximize your business growth and establish a solid reputation in the industry.

Chapter 9: Providing Exceptional Service

Chapter 9 emphasizes the importance of providing exceptional service to your clients. Satisfied clients are not only more likely to achieve their fitness goals but also become loyal advocates for your business. This chapter will explore the elements of exceptional service, including client assessments, personalized training programs, effective communication, and ongoing support. By going above and beyond for your clients, you can establish long-term relationships and ensure the success of your personal training business.

Chapter 10: Growing Your Personal Training Business

The final chapter, Chapter 10, focuses on strategies for growing your personal training business. As your business gains momentum, it's essential to continually expand your reach and increase your revenue streams. In this chapter, we'll discuss innovative techniques for scaling your business, diversifying your services, and staying ahead of trends in the fitness industry. Implementing these growth strategies will help you take your personal training business to new heights of success.

Now that you have a sneak peek of what's to come, let's get started on your journey to becoming a successful personal training entrepreneur!

Chapter 1: Introduction to Personal Training

Personal training is a dynamic and rewarding career choice, perfect for fitness enthusiasts who have a genuine passion for helping others achieve their health and fitness goals. If you love staying active, have a knack for motivating people, and want a career that's both challenging and fulfilling, personal training might just be the perfect fit for you. In this chapter, we'll dive into what personal training is all about, the crucial role personal trainers play, and the many benefits of pursuing this profession.

What is Personal Training?

So, what exactly is personal training? At its core, personal training is all about working one-on-one with individuals to create fitness programs tailored specifically to their needs and goals. As a personal trainer, your job is to guide and motivate your clients, teach them proper exercise techniques, and keep track of their progress. Whether your clients are looking to lose weight, build muscle, improve athletic performance, or simply boost their overall fitness, your expertise will help them get there.

Imagine being the person who helps someone transform their life, achieve their dreams, and reach new heights they never thought possible. That's the power of personal training.

The Role of a Personal Trainer

As a personal trainer, you'll wear many hats. You'll be a coach, an educator, a motivator, and sometimes even a confidant. Your primary responsibility is to design and implement workout programs that are safe, challenging, and aligned with your clients' goals.

You'll start by assessing each client's fitness level and understanding their objectives. From there, you'll create personalized plans that might include strength training, cardiovascular exercises, flexibility work, and more. But it doesn't stop there. You'll also need to monitor their progress, provide feedback, and adjust the program as needed to keep them on the right track.

Being a personal trainer means you're there every step of the way, cheering them on, pushing them when they need it, and celebrating their successes.

Benefits of Pursuing a Career in Personal Training

Choosing a career in personal training offers a host of benefits, both personally and professionally. Here are some of the top reasons why becoming a personal trainer can be such a fantastic career move:

1. Fulfilling and Rewarding

There's nothing quite like the feeling of helping someone improve their health and achieve their fitness goals. Watching your clients progress, seeing their confidence grow, and knowing that you played a key role in their journey is incredibly fulfilling. It's a job where you can truly make a difference in people's lives.

2. Flexibility and Independence

One of the biggest perks of being a personal trainer is the flexibility it offers. You can choose to work in a gym, open your own fitness studio, or even provide mobile training services. This flexibility allows you to create a work-life balance that suits your needs. Plus, being your own boss means you can set your own schedule and work with clients when it fits best for you.

3. Continuous Learning

The fitness industry is always evolving, with new research and techniques emerging all the time. As a personal trainer, you'll have the opportunity to stay updated with the latest scientific knowledge and continuously enhance your skills. Professional development courses and certifications can help you stay at the top of your game and provide the best possible service to your clients.

4. Financial Potential

With the growing focus on health and wellness, the demand for personal trainers is on the rise. This means there's excellent earning potential for dedicated and skilled professionals. As you build your client base and reputation, your income can increase significantly. The more successful your clients are, the more referrals and repeat business you'll get, which can lead to a thriving career.

5. Positive Impact on Health

Personal trainers play a crucial role in improving the health and wellbeing of individuals. By helping clients develop healthy habits, increase physical activity, and achieve their fitness goals, you contribute to reducing the prevalence of chronic diseases and promoting a healthier society. Your work can have a lasting impact not just on individual clients, but on the community as a whole.

In conclusion, personal training is an exciting and fulfilling profession that offers numerous benefits for both trainers and their clients. As we delve deeper into the topic, we'll explore how to assess your skills and qualifications to excel in this field. Whether you're just starting out or looking to take your career to the next level, this guide will provide you with the knowledge and tools you need to succeed.

Chapter 2: Assessing Your Skills and Qualifications

Starting a personal training business is an exciting venture, but it's crucial to start on the right foot. Assessing your skills and qualifications is the cornerstone of building a successful business. It helps you identify your strengths, uncover areas for improvement, and determine which clients you are best suited to help. Let's dive into the various aspects you need to consider when evaluating your skills and qualifications to set the stage for a thriving personal training business.

Evaluating Your Fitness Knowledge and Expertise

Before you hang out your shingle as a personal trainer, it's important to take a hard look at your fitness knowledge and expertise. Here are some questions to guide your self-assessment:

1. **Understanding of Exercise Physiology, Anatomy, and Nutrition:** How well do you grasp these core areas? This foundational knowledge is critical for creating effective and safe workout plans.
2. **Certifications and Qualifications:** Do you have any certifications in personal

training or related fields? Credentials from reputable organizations, like the National Academy of Sports Medicine (NASM) or the American Council on Exercise (ACE), can boost your credibility and show your dedication to the profession.

3. **Practical Experience:** Have you had hands-on experience in crafting workout plans and coaching individuals? Practical experience is invaluable and often separates successful trainers from the rest.

If you notice any gaps in your knowledge or qualifications, consider investing in further education or training. Certifications not only enhance your skills but also reassure clients of your expertise and professionalism.

Identifying Your Specializations

In the world of personal training, specialization can set you apart from the competition. Identifying your niche allows you to target specific markets and tailor your services to meet their unique needs. Think about these questions:

1. **Target Clients:** Are you drawn to working with specific groups like athletes, seniors, pregnant women, or individuals with particular medical conditions?
2. **Areas of Expertise:** Do you have a knack for weight loss, strength training, sports performance, or rehabilitation?

3. **Preferred Techniques:** Are there certain exercise modalities or techniques that you excel in or particularly enjoy?

By honing in on your specializations, you can carve out a niche market and become the go-to expert in that area, making your services highly sought after.

Assessing Your Communication and Interpersonal Skills

As a personal trainer, your ability to connect with clients is just as important as your fitness expertise. Reflect on these aspects of your communication and interpersonal skills:

1. **Active Listening:** Can you listen empathetically to your clients' needs and concerns?
2. **Clear Explanation:** Are you able to explain complex fitness concepts in a way that's easy for clients to understand?
3. **Motivational Skills:** Do you feel confident in motivating and challenging clients to reach their fitness goals?
4. **Approachability and Adaptability:** Are you approachable, and can you adapt your communication style to suit different clients?

If you find areas where you could improve, consider seeking out training or coaching. Effective communication is key to building strong client relationships and ensuring their success.

Understanding Business and Entrepreneurial Skills

Running a personal training business involves more than just fitness know-how. You'll need a solid grasp of various business and entrepreneurial skills. Here's what to consider:

1. **Financial Management:** Do you understand the basics of budgeting and pricing your services?
2. **Marketing Strategy:** Can you develop a marketing plan and effectively promote your services?
3. **Administrative Tasks:** Are you comfortable managing appointments, keeping client records, and handling invoices?
4. **Willingness to Learn:** Are you open to learning new business strategies and staying updated with industry trends?

If your business skills need a boost, think about taking relevant courses, attending workshops, or finding a business mentor. A strong foundation in business will help you navigate the challenges of running your own personal training enterprise.

Conclusion

Assessing your skills and qualifications is a vital step in launching a personal training business. By thoroughly evaluating your fitness knowledge, specializations, communication abilities, and business acumen, you can pinpoint areas for growth and understand the unique value you offer your clients. Remember, being a successful personal trainer is about more than just helping others achieve their fitness goals—it's also about your continuous development as a professional. So, take the time to assess where you stand, make necessary improvements, and set yourself up for a rewarding career in personal training.

Chapter 3: Understanding Your Target Market

Personal training enthusiasts! Today, let's dive into one of the most crucial aspects of building a successful personal training business: understanding your target market. This chapter is all about identifying the specific group of individuals who will most benefit from and be interested in your services. By getting to know your target market inside and out, you can tailor your marketing strategies, services, and communication to meet their unique needs and preferences.

Defining Your Niche

First things first, let's talk about defining your niche. In the vast world of personal training, having a niche means specializing in a specific area or demographic. This could be anything from weight loss and postnatal fitness to sports performance or senior fitness. When you clearly define your niche, you can focus your marketing efforts and develop expertise in that particular area. Think of it as carving out your own little corner of the personal training universe where you can truly shine.

Conducting Market Research

Next up, market research. This step is all about gathering information about your potential clients, competitors, and industry trends. It's like being a detective, uncovering all the details that will help you understand your target market's needs, preferences, and behaviors. You can use various research methods like online surveys, focus groups, or even one-on-one interviews with potential clients or industry experts. The goal is to gather data that provides insights into who your target market is and what they're looking for in a personal trainer.

Identifying Demographics

Now, let's get into demographics. Demographics are the statistical data that describe a population, including factors like age, gender, income, occupation, and education level. Knowing the demographics of your target market helps you create targeted marketing campaigns and tailor your services to meet their specific needs. For example, if your niche is prenatal fitness, you might be focusing on pregnant women in their 20s to 40s. Understanding these details allows you to connect with your audience on a deeper level.

Analyzing Psychographics

Moving on to psychographics. While demographics tell you who your target market is, psychographics delve deeper into their psychological and behavioral traits. This includes their interests, values, attitudes, and lifestyle choices. By analyzing psychographics, you can gain insights into what motivates your target market to pursue fitness goals. For instance, if your target market values sustainability and eco-friendly practices, you can incorporate these values into your fitness programs, making them more appealing to your audience.

Considering Geographic Factors

Geographic factors also play a role in understanding your target market. Think about the location of your potential clients and how it might impact their fitness goals and preferences. For example, if you operate in a suburban area with many families, your target market might include parents looking for family-oriented fitness programs. Understanding the geographic context helps you design services that are convenient and relevant to your clients' lifestyles.

Staying Updated with Industry Trends

Last but not least, keep an eye on industry trends. The fitness industry is always evolving, with new trends and innovations popping up regularly. Staying updated with these trends helps you understand the changing preferences and needs of your target market. By staying ahead of the curve, you can position yourself as a knowledgeable and innovative personal trainer, always offering the latest and greatest to your clients.

Putting It All Together

Understanding your target market is key to the success of your personal training business. It allows you to tailor your services, marketing efforts, and communication to effectively reach and engage your ideal clients. By continually assessing and analyzing your target market, you can adapt and refine your approach to ensure you're meeting their evolving needs and preferences.

Take the time to conduct thorough market research, define your niche, and understand both the demographics and psychographics of your target market. This investment in understanding your audience will pay off in the long run, enabling you to build strong, lasting relationships with your clients and provide them with the personalized fitness experience they desire.

Remember, personal training is all about helping individuals achieve their fitness goals. By understanding your target market, you can position yourself as the go-to personal trainer for their needs and make a positive impact on their health and well-being. So, get out there, do your research, and start connecting with your ideal clients today!

Chapter 4: Developing Your Business Plan

Starting a personal training business is an exciting venture, but it requires careful planning and strategic decision-making. One of the most crucial steps in this process is developing a solid business plan. Think of your business plan as your roadmap, outlining your goals, strategies, and financial projections. It gives you a clear direction and helps you stay focused on your objectives.

Why Do You Need a Business Plan?

A well-crafted business plan is essential for several reasons:

1. **Defining Your Mission and Vision**: It helps you articulate your business's mission, vision, and values. This process forces you to think critically about what sets your personal training business apart from competitors and how you plan to serve your clients. By clarifying your unique selling proposition, you can better position your business in the market and attract your target audience.
2. **Assessing Financial Feasibility**: A business plan helps you evaluate the financial aspects of your venture. It allows

you to outline your startup costs, projected revenue streams, and operating expenses. This financial analysis provides a realistic picture of how much money you need to invest initially and how long it will take to break even and start generating profits.
3. **Attracting Investors and Securing Financing**: Whether you plan to seek funding from a bank, private investors, or government grants, having a detailed business plan demonstrates your professionalism, commitment, and potential for success. It shows that you have thoroughly researched your market, understand your target audience, and have a well-thought-out strategy for growth.

Key Components of a Business Plan

Let's break down the key components of a comprehensive business plan:

1. **Executive Summary**: This section provides an overview of your business, including your mission, keys to success, and goals. It's like the trailer to your business plan, designed to grab the reader's attention and summarize the main points.
2. **Company Description**: Here, you describe your personal training business in detail. Include information about your services, target market, competitive advantages, and location. This is where you

paint the picture of what your business is all about.

3. **Market Analysis**: Conduct thorough market research to understand your target market, industry trends, and competitors. Identify your niche and explain how you plan to differentiate yourself in the market. This section shows you know your stuff and have a strategy to stand out.

4. **Organization and Management**: Outline the structure of your business, including the roles and responsibilities of key team members. Mention any strategic partnerships or collaborations you have established. This gives insight into who's running the show and how the business is organized.

5. **Products and Services**: Provide a comprehensive overview of the services you offer, including pricing, packages, and any specialized programs or certifications you hold. This section showcases what you're bringing to the table.

6. **Marketing and Sales**: Describe your marketing strategies, including online and offline channels, social media, advertising, and promotions. Explain how you plan to attract and retain clients. This part is crucial for showing how you'll get and keep customers.

7. **Financial Projections**: Present your financial forecasts, including revenue projections, startup costs, and operating expenses. Include a break-even analysis and demonstrate that your business is

financially viable. This section reassures that your numbers add up.
8. **Implementation Plan**: Detail how you plan to execute your strategies and achieve your goals. Include timelines, milestones, and key performance indicators to track your progress. This is your action plan, showing how you'll turn ideas into reality.

Updating and Revising Your Business Plan

A business plan is not a static document. It should be regularly reviewed and updated as your business evolves. As you gain experience and insights, you may need to adjust your strategies or target market. Additionally, changes in the industry or economic conditions may require you to revise your financial projections.

Continuously monitoring and evaluating your business plan ensures that you stay on track and adapt to changing circumstances. Regularly reviewing your goals, performance metrics, and market trends allows you to make informed decisions and seize new opportunities.

In conclusion, developing a comprehensive business plan is a critical step in starting and growing your personal training business. It helps you clarify your goals, assess your financial feasibility, attract investors, and guide your day-to-day operations. By dedicating time and effort to developing a well-thought-out plan, you can set yourself up for success in the competitive personal training industry. So, take the plunge and start drafting your business plan—your future self will thank you!

Chapter 5: Legal and Regulatory Considerations

Running a personal training business isn't just about helping clients achieve their health and fitness goals. There's a whole legal and regulatory side to it that you need to be aware of to keep your business on the right track. In this chapter, we'll explore the key considerations and steps you need to take to ensure your business operates within the law and meets all necessary regulations.

Understanding Legal Structures

Before you dive into the world of personal training, it's important to figure out the best legal structure for your business. You have several options, including sole proprietorship, partnership, limited liability company (LLC), and corporation. Each of these structures has its own pros and cons in terms of liability, taxation, and management.

For instance, a sole proprietorship is the simplest form and gives you complete control, but it also means you're personally liable for any debts or legal actions. An LLC, on the other hand, offers protection against personal liability, but it might come with more paperwork and fees. To make an informed decision, it's a good idea to consult with a legal professional or accountant who can guide you based on your specific circumstances.

Obtaining Licenses and Permits

In many places, you don't need a specific license to practice as a personal trainer. However, it's crucial to check your local and state regulations to ensure you're in compliance with any licensing requirements that might apply. Additionally, if you plan to operate a fitness facility, you might need to obtain certain permits or certifications.

This step is essential to avoid any legal hassles down the line. It's better to invest some time upfront to understand and meet all regulatory requirements rather than facing potential fines or business interruptions later.

Insurance Coverage

Insurance is a vital aspect of running a personal training business. It helps protect you and your clients from potential risks and liabilities. There are a few types of insurance you should consider:

1. **Professional Liability Insurance**: Also known as errors and omissions insurance, this covers claims made against you for alleged negligence, injury, or damage.
2. **General Liability Insurance**: This covers accidents or damage that may occur on your premises.
3. **Health Insurance**: If you have employees, you might need to provide health insurance as part of their benefits package.

Having adequate insurance coverage is like having a safety net for your business. It ensures that you can handle unexpected events without severe financial repercussions.

Client Agreements and Waivers

To protect your business and establish clear expectations with your clients, it's essential to have well-drafted client agreements and liability waivers. These documents should outline the terms and conditions of your services, define client responsibilities, and address any potential risks associated with fitness training.

It's advisable to consult with a legal professional to ensure these agreements are comprehensive, enforceable, and comply with relevant laws and regulations. Clear and thorough documentation can prevent misunderstandings and protect you in case of any disputes.

Data Protection and Privacy

As a personal trainer, you'll likely collect and store sensitive personal information from your clients, such as medical history and contact details. It's crucial to prioritize data protection and privacy by implementing secure systems and practices.

Familiarize yourself with applicable privacy laws and regulations, such as the General Data Protection Regulation (GDPR) if you operate in the European Union. Be transparent about how you collect, use, store, and share clients' personal information and obtain their consent accordingly. This not only builds trust with your clients but also keeps you compliant with legal standards.

Employee and Contractor Considerations

If you plan to hire employees or engage independent contractors to work with you, it's important to fully understand and comply with employment and labor laws. This includes adhering to minimum wage requirements, providing appropriate benefits, and ensuring workplace safety.

Consult with an employment attorney or HR professional to ensure you are meeting all legal obligations related to hiring and managing staff. Properly managing these aspects can help you avoid legal issues and create a positive work environment.

Tax Compliance

Maintaining accurate financial records and complying with tax obligations is essential for any business. As a personal trainer, you may be subject to different tax requirements depending on your legal structure and the jurisdiction in which you operate.

Consider hiring a qualified accountant or tax professional to assist you in understanding your tax obligations, filing taxes correctly, and maximizing any available deductions. This can save you time and stress, allowing you to focus more on your clients and less on paperwork.

Professional Associations and Code of Ethics

Joining professional associations in the fitness industry can provide you with valuable resources, networking opportunities, and continuing education options. Many of these associations have their own code of ethics that members must adhere to.

Familiarize yourself with these codes and strive to uphold the highest professional standards in your personal training practice. Being part of a professional community not only enhances your credibility but also keeps you informed about industry trends and best practices.

Conclusion

Understanding and complying with legal and regulatory considerations is essential for the success and longevity of your personal training business. Taking the time to familiarize yourself with the relevant laws, obtaining necessary licenses and permits, maintaining sufficient insurance coverage, and implementing proper agreements and policies will help protect your business, clients, and reputation.

Stay informed about any changes in regulations and seek legal guidance when needed to ensure your business remains compliant and operates within the legal boundaries. By covering all these bases, you'll set a strong foundation for your personal training business and pave the way for long-term success.

Chapter 6: Setting Up Your Business Operations

Setting up your personal training business is a significant step toward achieving your professional goals. It's not just about having the right equipment or finding the perfect location; it's about creating an environment where your clients feel comfortable, safe, and motivated. Let's explore the essential aspects of setting up your business operations.

Setting Up Your Physical Space

Location

Choosing the right location is crucial. Think about your target market and what would be convenient for them. Is it easy to get to? Is there plenty of parking? How about access to public transportation? And don't forget to check the zoning regulations in your area to make sure you're compliant with local laws.

Layout and Equipment

Your gym layout should maximize the use of space and ensure safety. Plan your space to allow for a variety of exercises without crowding. Depending on your clients' needs, you'll need essential equipment like dumbbells, resistance bands, stability balls, and cardio machines. Consider investing in versatile, high-quality equipment that will stand the test of time.

Safety and Hygiene

Safety and cleanliness are paramount. Ensure your space is well-lit and properly ventilated. Choose flooring that reduces the risk of injury and is easy to clean. Establish a rigorous cleaning protocol, especially for high-touch areas and shared equipment. Clear, visible safety instructions will help your clients feel confident and informed.

Technology and Software

Incorporating technology can streamline your operations significantly. Fitness tracking apps, scheduling software, and client management systems can help you keep track of client progress, manage appointments, and handle administrative tasks efficiently. Automating these processes saves time and allows you to focus more on training.

Creating Policies and Procedures

Scheduling and Cancellations

Define your business hours and make your availability clear to your clients. Establish a cancellation policy to manage no-shows or last-minute cancellations. Clearly communicate this policy to avoid misunderstandings.

Payment and Pricing

Decide how you will accept payments – cash, credit/debit cards, or online platforms. Determine your pricing based on session length, your level of expertise, and any additional services. Be upfront about your rates and payment terms to ensure transparency.

Client Intake and Assessment

A standardized client intake process is essential. Gather necessary information such as medical history, fitness goals, and previous exercise experience. Conduct fitness assessments to set baseline measurements and track progress over time.

Health and Safety

Set clear health and safety protocols. This includes warm-up and cool-down procedures, proper technique instructions, and hygiene practices.

Emphasize the importance of hydration and using safety equipment.

Hiring and Training Staff

As your business grows, you might need to hire staff. Here's what to consider:

Qualifications and Expertise

Look for candidates with relevant certifications and experience in the fitness industry. They should have a solid understanding of exercise principles, safety protocols, and client management.

Cultural Fit

Seek out individuals who share your passion for fitness and align with your business values. A positive, motivating attitude is essential in creating a supportive environment for clients.

Training and Development

Provide ongoing training and development opportunities for your staff. Encourage them to stay updated with industry trends and continue their education through workshops and certifications.

Communication and Collaboration

Ensure your staff can communicate effectively with both you and your clients. Emphasize the importance of building strong client relationships and delivering exceptional customer service.

Delegation and Supervision

Clearly define roles and responsibilities to avoid confusion. Set up a system for supervising and evaluating staff performance to maintain high-quality services.

Administration and Documentation

Efficient administration is the backbone of any successful business. Here are some key areas to focus on:

Client Records

Maintain accurate records for each client, including contact information, health history, progress notes, and consent forms. Use a secure system to store and access these records.

Financial Management

Organize your finances meticulously. Track expenses, invoice clients promptly, and keep accurate income records. Consider hiring an accountant or using accounting software to manage your finances and ensure compliance with tax obligations.

Marketing and Promotions

A robust marketing strategy will help attract new clients and retain existing ones. Create a professional website and establish a strong social media presence to showcase your services and client testimonials. Consider offering promotions, referral programs, and loyalty rewards to engage your clients.

Client Communication

Regular communication with your clients is key. Keep them informed about updates, promotions, or upcoming events through newsletters, social media, and personalized messages. Building a sense of community will foster client loyalty.

Legal and Compliance

Ensure your business complies with all legal and regulatory requirements. Adhere to privacy laws when handling client information. Consult with legal professionals to draft contracts, agreements, and liability waivers to protect your business.

By meticulously setting up your business operations, you create an environment conducive to delivering exceptional service and achieving success in the personal training industry. Prioritize safety, efficiency, and client satisfaction in every aspect of your operations.

Chapter 7: Building Your Brand and Online Presence

Personal trainers! Congratulations on setting up your personal training business. Now it's time to take things to the next level by building your brand and creating a compelling online presence. In today's digital age, having a strong online presence is essential for attracting clients and growing your business. Let's dive into how you can make your brand stand out and establish a remarkable online presence.

The Importance of Branding

When we talk about branding, it's more than just a logo and a catchy tagline. Branding is about the overall perception and reputation of your personal training business. Your brand should reflect your values, personality, and unique selling proposition. Effective branding helps you stand out from the competition and increases your credibility with your target market.

Think about what makes you different from other personal trainers. Is it your expertise, specialization, or unique approach to fitness? This uniqueness is the foundation of your brand identity. Clearly communicate this across all your marketing materials and online platforms to build a recognizable and trustworthy brand.

Creating a Compelling Brand Identity

Creating a compelling brand identity starts with defining your brand's core elements. Ask yourself: What is your mission as a personal trainer? What vision do you have for your business? What values do you hold dear? These answers will help shape your brand identity.

Next, design a logo that aligns with your brand's personality and values. Your logo should be visually appealing, memorable, and easily recognizable. Consider working with a professional graphic designer to create a logo that truly represents your brand. Alongside your logo, choose a color palette and font combination that you'll consistently use in all your marketing materials. Consistency in visual elements creates a cohesive and professional look for your brand.

Creating a Professional Website

With your brand identity in place, it's time to establish an online presence through a professional website. Your website is the central hub where potential clients learn more about your services and make inquiries. Make sure your website is user-friendly, visually appealing, and mobile-responsive.

Include essential information like your background and qualifications, the services you offer, client testimonials, and contact information. Adding a blog section is a great idea too. Regularly sharing educational and informative content related to fitness and health not only showcases your expertise but also helps drive traffic to your website through search engine optimization (SEO).

Utilizing Social Media

Social media platforms are powerful tools for building your brand and connecting with potential clients. Create accounts on popular platforms like Facebook, Instagram, and Twitter, and regularly post engaging and relevant content. Share fitness tips, success stories, client testimonials, and before-and-after photos to showcase your expertise.

Engage with your audience by responding to comments and messages promptly. This builds trust and fosters a loyal following. Consider collaborating with influencers or fitness enthusiasts who align with your brand to expand your reach. Partnering with influencers can expose your brand to a wider audience and attract more potential clients.

Online Advertising and Marketing

Beyond organic social media content, investing in online advertising and marketing strategies can further promote your personal training business. Platforms like Google Ads and Facebook Ads allow you to target specific demographics and interests, ensuring your advertisements reach your ideal clients.

Content marketing is another effective strategy. Creating and sharing informative blog posts or videos can attract potential clients and establish you as a thought leader in the industry. The more valuable content you provide, the more likely people will see you as a trusted expert.

Monitoring and Maintaining Your Online Presence

Building your brand and online presence is an ongoing process. Regularly monitor your online platforms for reviews, comments, and messages. Respond to any feedback—positive or negative—in a professional and timely manner. Consistently update your website and social media profiles with fresh content to keep your audience engaged.

Stay informed about the latest trends and tools in digital marketing to stay ahead of the competition. Remember, your online presence should always align with your brand identity and mission. A strong and authentic brand will help you attract and retain clients while solidifying your position as a trusted personal trainer.

Conclusion

Building a brand and establishing an online presence is essential for the success of your personal training business. By defining your brand identity, creating a professional website, utilizing social media, and implementing online advertising strategies, you can effectively reach your target market and build a strong client base. Remember to maintain and monitor your online presence regularly to ensure your brand remains consistent and resonates with your audience.

So, get out there and start building your brand! Your future clients are waiting to connect with you online.

Chapter 8: Acquiring Clients and Networking

Building a successful personal training business hinges on having a steady stream of clients. Acquiring clients and effective networking are essential steps to ensure the growth and sustainability of your business. In this chapter, we'll explore various strategies and techniques to help you attract and retain clients and build a strong network within the fitness industry.

Identifying Your Ideal Client

Before diving into client acquisition, it's crucial to identify your ideal client. Think about the specific demographic and psychographic characteristics that align with your expertise and specialization. Are you targeting athletes, busy professionals, seniors, or individuals looking to lose weight? Understanding your ideal client will allow you to tailor your marketing efforts to reach the right audience.

For example, if your specialty is helping busy professionals stay fit, your marketing message should highlight quick yet effective workout routines that fit into a hectic schedule. On the other hand, if you focus on seniors, emphasize safe, low-impact exercises designed to improve mobility and overall health. By honing in on your ideal client, you can create more targeted and compelling marketing messages.

Referrals and Word-of-Mouth Marketing

One of the most effective ways to acquire clients is through referrals and word-of-mouth marketing. Satisfied clients are more likely to recommend your services to their friends, family, and colleagues. To encourage referrals, you can offer incentives such as a discounted session or a referral bonus. Additionally, make sure to provide exceptional service to every client, as positive experiences will naturally lead to organic referrals.

Consider developing a referral program that rewards clients who bring in new business. For instance, offer a free session for every three new clients they refer or a discounted rate on their next package. Personal recommendations carry significant weight, so fostering a referral-friendly environment can significantly boost your client base.

Networking within the Fitness Industry

Networking within the fitness industry can help you establish valuable connections and collaborations. Attend industry conferences, trade shows, and seminars to meet other fitness professionals, gym owners, and potential clients. Join professional associations and organizations to enhance your credibility and expand your network. Building relationships with other professionals in your field can lead to client referrals and partnership opportunities.

For instance, you might meet a local gym owner who is willing to refer clients to you, or a nutritionist who needs a trusted personal trainer to recommend to their clients. Networking can also provide insights into industry trends and best practices, helping you stay ahead of the curve.

Online Marketing and Social Media

In today's digital age, online marketing and social media play a crucial role in acquiring clients. Create a professional website that showcases your expertise, services, and testimonials. Optimize your website for search engines to increase your online visibility. Utilize social media platforms such as Facebook, Instagram, and Twitter to engage with potential clients, share fitness tips, and success stories. Consider running targeted online advertising campaigns to reach your ideal client demographic.

Your online presence should reflect your brand and expertise. Regularly post content that demonstrates your knowledge and engages your audience, such as workout videos, client testimonials, and fitness tips. Respond to comments and messages promptly to build relationships and trust with potential clients.

Offering Introductory Sessions and Promotions

To attract new clients, consider offering introductory sessions or promotions. This allows potential clients to experience your services firsthand and see the value you provide. Provide a discounted rate for the first session or offer a package deal for new clients. Additionally, offer promotions during holidays or special occasions to incentivize potential clients to try out your services.

For example, a "New Year, New You" promotion offering a discount on your training packages can attract clients looking to start their fitness journey at the beginning of the year. Introductory offers lower the barrier to entry, making it easier for potential clients to commit to your services.

Collaborating with Local Businesses

Partnering with local businesses can be a win-win situation for both parties involved. Identify complementary businesses such as nutritionists, chiropractors, or wellness centers, and explore collaboration opportunities. For example, you can offer joint workshops or referral discounts. This not only expands your client base but also boosts your credibility within the community.

Consider setting up referral arrangements where you and the local business mutually benefit. For instance, a chiropractor could refer their patients to you for fitness training, while you could send your clients to them for chiropractic care. Collaborations can create a supportive network that benefits everyone involved.

Building a Strong Online Presence

In addition to your website and social media channels, leverage online platforms and directories dedicated to connecting trainers with clients. Register your business on fitness directories and review sites where potential clients can find and assess your services. Encourage satisfied clients to leave positive reviews to enhance your online reputation.

Positive reviews are incredibly influential in the decision-making process for potential clients. Regularly check these platforms and respond to reviews to show that you value client feedback and are committed to providing excellent service.

Providing Exceptional Customer Service

Finally, remember that providing exceptional customer service is crucial for client acquisition and retention. Listen to your clients' needs, goals, and concerns, and tailor your training programs accordingly. Regularly check in with your clients to assess progress and make adjustments. Going above and beyond for your clients will not only help you retain them but also lead to positive recommendations and referrals.

Exceptional customer service means being attentive, responsive, and genuinely invested in your clients' success. Personalize your approach to each client, celebrate their milestones, and provide ongoing support to help them achieve their goals.

Conclusion

Acquiring clients and networking are essential components of building a successful personal training business. Develop a strong referral system, network within the fitness industry, utilize online marketing strategies, offer introductory sessions and promotions, collaborate with local businesses, and focus on providing exceptional customer service. By implementing these strategies, you'll attract and retain clients, ultimately growing your personal training business. Now, get out there, make those connections, and watch your business thrive!

Chapter 9: Providing Exceptional Service

In the world of personal training, providing exceptional service is your ticket to building a successful and thriving business. Clients are looking for more than just a workout; they want personalized attention, expert guidance, and a positive experience throughout their fitness journey. When you go above and beyond their expectations, you can create loyal clients who will not only stick with you but also refer you to their friends and family. Let's dive into how you can provide that exceptional service.

Understanding Your Clients

To truly provide exceptional service, you need to have a deep understanding of your clients. This means going beyond just knowing their fitness goals and exercise preferences. Take the time to learn about their individual needs, limitations, and motivations. Ask open-ended questions and really listen to their responses. This will allow you to create customized workouts and make appropriate adjustments as needed.

For example, if a client mentions that they have a knee injury, you'll know to avoid high-impact exercises and instead focus on low-impact alternatives that won't aggravate their condition. By showing that you care about their specific situation, you build trust and rapport, which are essential for a lasting client-trainer relationship.

Creating Personalized Fitness Programs

One of the key ways to provide exceptional service is by creating personalized fitness programs for each client. Tailor the workouts based on their goals, abilities, and any specific health considerations they may have. Incorporate a variety of exercises to keep them engaged and challenged. Regularly assess their progress and modify the program accordingly.

For instance, if a client wants to improve their cardiovascular health, mix up their routine with different cardio activities like running, cycling, and swimming. This variety not only keeps things interesting but also ensures a well-rounded fitness regimen. By doing so, you'll demonstrate your expertise and show your clients that you are genuinely invested in their success.

Being Professional and Punctual

Professionalism and punctuality are crucial when it comes to providing exceptional service. Always arrive on time for sessions and come prepared with a well-structured workout plan. Dress appropriately and maintain a positive and respectful attitude. Show genuine interest in your clients' well-being and be attentive throughout the session.

Your professionalism will instill confidence and trust in your clients. They'll see you as a reliable and dedicated professional who takes their fitness journey seriously. This level of commitment goes a long way in building a strong, lasting relationship with your clients.

Offering Motivation and Accountability

Motivation is often the key to a client's success. Be their cheerleader and provide constant encouragement. Celebrate their milestones and achievements, no matter how small they may seem. Keep them motivated by setting realistic goals, tracking progress, and providing positive feedback.

Additionally, hold them accountable by following up on their commitments and ensuring they are consistently putting in effort towards their fitness goals. For example, if a client struggles with sticking to their workout routine, check in with them regularly and offer tips to stay on track. Your support and accountability can make all the difference in their fitness journey.

Continuing Education and Professional Development

To stay at the top of your field and provide exceptional service, you must continuously educate yourself and seek professional development opportunities. Stay updated on the latest research, trends, and best practices in the fitness industry. Attend workshops, seminars, and conferences to enhance your skills and knowledge.

By investing in your own growth, you can offer innovative and effective training methods to your clients. For instance, learning about the latest advancements in functional training can help you introduce new exercises that are both effective and exciting for your clients.

Building Strong Relationships

Building strong relationships with your clients is crucial for providing exceptional service. Take the time to get to know them on a personal level and show genuine care and interest in their well-being. Remember important details about their lives and interests, and use this information to make their experience more personalized.

Regularly check in with them outside of training sessions to see how they are progressing and offer support. By building strong relationships, you create a sense of loyalty and trust with your clients, making them more likely to stick with you in the long run.

Seeking and Incorporating Feedback

Feedback is invaluable in improving your service and meeting your clients' needs. Encourage your clients to provide feedback on their experiences and listen openly to their suggestions and concerns. Actively seek ways to improve and make necessary adjustments to your training methods or service offerings.

For instance, if a client mentions that they would like more variety in their workouts, take that feedback seriously and incorporate new exercises into their routine. By doing so, you demonstrate that you value their opinions and are dedicated to continuously improving their experience.

Conclusion

Providing exceptional service is the key to standing out in the personal training industry. By understanding your clients, creating personalized fitness programs, being professional and punctual, offering motivation and accountability, continuing your education, building strong relationships, and seeking feedback, you can deliver a service that exceeds expectations. Remember, exceptional service not only leads to client satisfaction and retention but also to positive referrals and a thriving business.

So, go ahead and put these principles into practice. Your clients will thank you, and your business will flourish as a result.

Chapter 10: Growing Your Personal Training Business

Expanding your personal training business is an exciting milestone that signals the growth of your brand and the effectiveness of your services. As you establish a solid foundation and attract clients, it's crucial to focus on strategies that will help you scale your business and reach a broader audience. Let's dive into some effective techniques and tactics to grow your personal training business successfully.

Enhance Your Services

One of the first steps in growing your personal training business is to continually enhance and diversify your services. Staying up-to-date with the latest fitness trends, attending workshops or conferences, and obtaining additional certifications can significantly broaden your expertise. This not only allows you to offer a wider range of services but also positions you as a knowledgeable and versatile trainer.

Consider introducing specialty programs like group fitness classes, boot camps, or online coaching. These new offerings can attract clients with diverse preferences and fitness goals. Additionally, creating packages or bundles can encourage clients to commit to longer-term programs, boosting your revenue and improving client retention.

Referrals and Testimonials

Word-of-mouth marketing is incredibly powerful for personal trainers. Happy clients are often eager to refer their friends, family, or colleagues to you. To encourage this, you can implement a referral program where clients receive incentives, such as discounted sessions or free training, for bringing in new clients.

Testimonials are another effective way to showcase the success and value of your services. Request feedback from your satisfied clients and ask if you can feature their testimonials on your website or social media platforms. Positive reviews and success stories build credibility and attract potential clients, demonstrating the tangible results of your training.

Collaborate with Others

Building collaborations with other professionals or businesses in the fitness industry can significantly expand your network. Partner with local gyms, fitness studios, health clubs, or wellness centers. You could offer to conduct classes or workshops at their facilities or collaborate on joint marketing campaigns. These partnerships can lead to cross-promotion and referrals, benefiting both parties.

Consider also collaborating with professionals in related fields, such as nutritionists, physical therapists, or chiropractors. These partnerships can help you offer a more holistic approach to health and wellness, providing comprehensive solutions to your clients and expanding your referral network.

Online Marketing and Social Media

In today's digital age, a strong online presence is vital for growing your personal training business. Use social media platforms like Instagram, Facebook, and YouTube to showcase your expertise, share fitness tips, and engage with your target audience. Regularly post content that is informative, visually appealing, and relevant to your clients' interests.

Invest in online advertising strategies, such as targeted Facebook or Instagram ads, to reach a broader audience. Create compelling and eye-catching ads that highlight the benefits of your services and explain why potential clients should choose you as their personal trainer.

Expand Your Network

Networking is an invaluable tool for business growth. Attend industry events, conferences, or workshops to connect with other fitness professionals and potential clients. Introduce yourself, exchange business cards, and take the opportunity to learn from others in the industry.

Building relationships with influencers or fitness enthusiasts can also help expand your network. Reach out to individuals with a large following on social media to collaborate on content or promotions. Their endorsement can introduce your services to a wider audience and attract new clients.

Continuously Improve Customer Service

Exceptional customer service is crucial for client satisfaction and retention. Focus on improving your communication skills, responsiveness, and attentiveness to your clients' needs. Ensure that each client feels valued and supported in their fitness journey. Regularly seek feedback to identify areas for improvement and address any concerns. Incorporate their suggestions to enhance your services and overall customer experience.

Conclusion

Growing your personal training business involves a combination of enhancing your services, leveraging referrals and testimonials, collaborating with others, utilizing online marketing strategies, expanding your network, and continuously improving customer service. By implementing these strategies, you can attract new clients, retain existing ones, and position your business for long-term success. With dedication and strategic planning, your personal training business can thrive and make a significant impact in the fitness industry.

www.ingramcontent.com/pod-product-compliance
Lightning Source LLC
Chambersburg PA
CBHW070133230526
45472CB00004B/1524